IMAGES
of America

THE TOWNS OF THE
MONADNOCK REGION

Playing croquet in Jaffrey some time before 1875 when the first Granite State Hotel, seen at the rear, was destroyed by fire. (JHS)

IMAGES
of America

THE TOWNS OF THE MONADNOCK REGION

Drawn mainly from the collections of the historical societies of
Dublin, Fitzwilliam, Hancock, Jaffrey,
Marlborough, New Ipswich, Peterborough and Rindge;
also, Historic Harrisville, Inc.
Additional photographs from private collections.

Compiled by
Robert B. Stephenson

ARCADIA
PUBLISHING

Copyright © 1994 by Robert B. Stephenson
ISBN 978-1-5316-4173-3

Published by Arcadia Publishing
Charleston, South Carolina

Library of Congress Catalog Card Number: 2008940192

For all general information contact Arcadia Publishing at:
Telephone 843-853-2070
Fax 843-853-0044
E-mail sales@arcadiapublishing.com
For customer service and orders:
Toll-Free 1-888-313-2665

Visit us on the Internet at www.arcadiapublishing.com

Other recent publications by Robert B. Stephenson:
Jaffrey Then and Now: Changes in Community Character (with Catherine L. Seiberling), 1994.

Dedicated to my mother, New Hampshire born and bred.

Contents

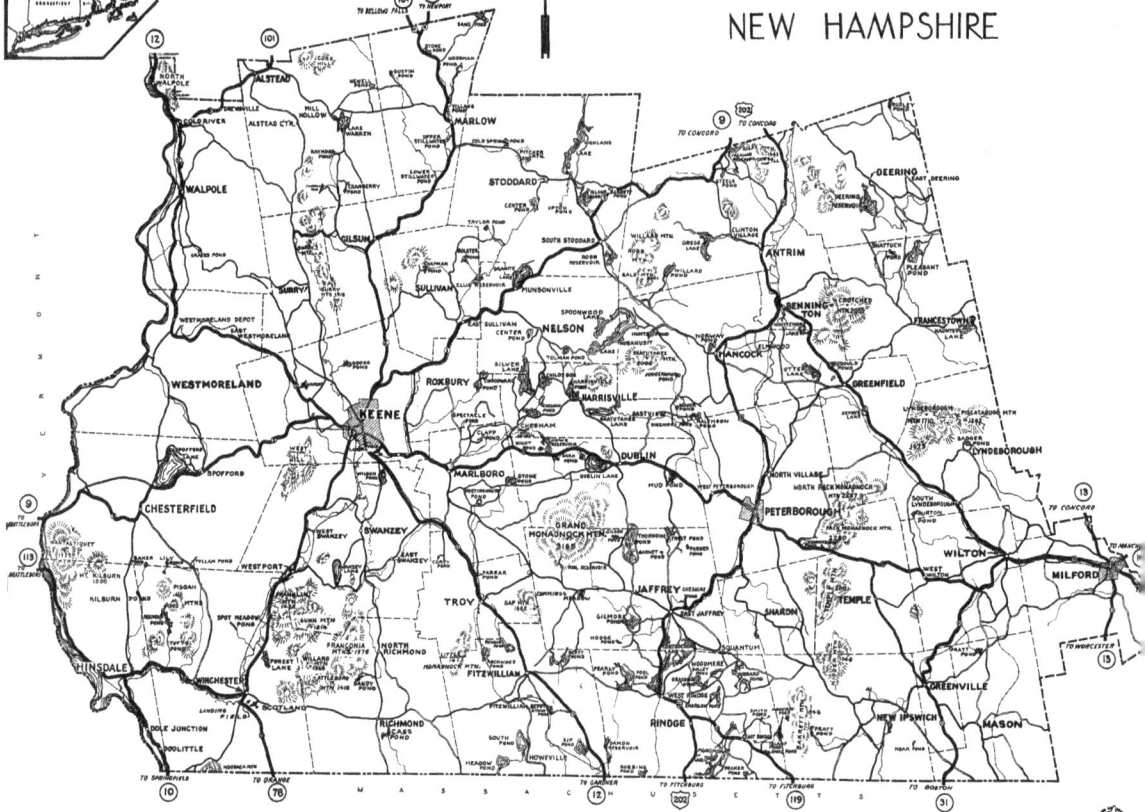

A map of the Monadnock Region prepared in 1936 by the New Hampshire State Planning and Development Commission. (RBS)

Introduction

Every historical society has a collection of old photographs. It may reside in a shoe box in the back of a cupboard, be nicely mounted and labeled in white ink in those black-page scrapbooks or—one can only hope—be expertly catalogued, precisely dated, accurately described, profusely documented and permanently protected for posterity in archival quality folders (and, of course, stored at the proper temperature and humidity).

The photographic collections of the local historical societies in the Monadnock region do, indeed, run this gamut. All share, however, at least one quality: they tell us how things were in earlier times. Invariably, the old images I'm most drawn to are the ones that pre-date me and are of scenes recognizable today. These are the ones that have lessons to tell. How did a street or a building change over time and was the change for the best?

Anyone who pores through hundreds of stereoscopic views of the 1860s and postcards of the 1930s—and everything in between—quickly realizes that certain themes recur frequently. That they do suggests what was thought noteworthy by our forebears: Mount Monadnock, of course; also the village and its mix of ingredients (the meetinghouse, the common, the post office and store, the inn, Main Street); work and play; public occasions and celebrations; catastrophe and disaster; and the ever-changing means of getting from here to there. The structure of this book simply reflects these recurring themes.

Regions are quite often artificial creations. The Monadnock region really is a region; its residents think of it as a region and refer to it as such. There are certain shared attributes relating to the landscape, history and culture of the area. The most obvious, of course, is the mountain itself, which, even if never climbed or not always noticed, is powerfully ever-present. Count the listings in the phone book if you doubt the spell of Monadnock. But it's a region that has indefinite boundaries. It starts at the mountain and works its way outward, but where does it end? It's hard to say (in compiling this book, several more communities might easily have been added and with justification). Being part of a region and sharing certain characteristics does not necessarily mean uniformity, however. The towns of the Monadnock region each have their distinctive identities. There are differences in architecture and townscape, in the types of business and industry, in the interests and lifestyles of the citizens and particularly in such subtle things as character and sense of place. Three good examples are Peterborough, Jaffrey and Rindge; three neighbors, each with about the same number of inhabitants but very different in so many other ways.

For an area so close to the coastal cities of Massachusetts and New Hampshire, the Monadnock region was settled relatively late, in the mid-1700s, long after some areas further inland. In 1736 a township called Rowley Canada was granted by the Great and General Court of the Province of Massachusetts to soldiers— or to their descendants—who had served in the Canada expedition of 1690. Most of the sixty-two grantees were from Rowley and neighboring towns, hence the name. When laid out, the township included much of what is now Jaffrey, Rindge and Sharon as well as small portions of Dublin and New Ipswich. Little in the way of permanent settlement resulted. Matters were clouded when the jurisdiction of Massachusetts over Rowley Canada was challenged by twelve prominent New Hampshire men, the majority from Portsmouth, who had purchased the original land grant made in 1620 by King James I to Captain John Mason. Known as the Masonian Proprietors, these twelve operated, according to the custom then, as a speculative land company. Most never saw the townships that resulted, which had the names Monadnock No. 1, No. 2 and so on. Later these future towns were to take on the names we know today: Rindge, Jaffrey, Dublin, Fitzwilliam and Marlborough (and some others as well). Although the dispute was settled in 1748 it didn't, in a sense, make a great deal of difference because virtually no permanent settlement had occurred up to then anyway. But soon things began to happen.

The history of how the region developed starting with the slow trickle of the Scotch-Irish pioneers in the 1750s and continuing through the boom of fleeing urbanites in the 1980s is a long and interesting one; too long to do justice to here. But the old photographs in this book perhaps give some sense of how it all happened, the difficulties encountered and the obstacles overcome.

Robert B. Stephenson
Jaffrey, New Hampshire

Note: The initials in parentheses at the close of each caption indicate the source of the photograph. Refer to the acknowledgments on page 128 for identification.

One

The Mountain

Mount Monadnock is what gives the Monadnock region in southwestern New Hampshire its name. Even before the earliest settlements in the eighteenth century it was a strong physical, spiritual and symbolic presence. The name is Algonquin in origin but there is little agreement about its translation. One source gives it as "the place of the unexcelled mountain." Monadnock has many historical and literary associations: Thoreau, Emerson, Twain, Whittier and Kipling all knew the mountain and referred to it in their works. It is, of course, a favorite of hikers, to such an extent that it is considered the most climbed mountain in the world. This view of Monadnock from Perry's Hill in Fitzwilliam is from a time (1898) when the forests had yet to reclaim the fields and meadows of an agricultural age. (FHS)

Monadnock may be approached from many directions. This group is accepting the challenge from the Dublin side, possibly on Farmer's (now the Dublin) Trail, *c.* 1905. (DHS)

This scene at the summit in the 1860s shows a particularly well-dressed party contemplating the view. Note the telescope. (JHS)

The first Mountain House was built on the south flank of Monadnock in 1860 by Moses Cudworth. It was a modest affair; however, in 1866, a new three-and-a-half-story building was opened. Among the guests that season were Ralph Waldo Emerson and William Ellery Channing. Unfortunately it burned to the ground that fall and the next year was replaced by this smaller version. (JHS)

The small replacement structure was added to and expanded several times. The date of this view, showing the approach along the Toll Road, is before 1885, when the hotel was topped off with a mansard roof. (JHS)

The Mountain House prior to 1885. Guests usually came by train and were met at the Troy depot and brought by carriage to the hotel. In 1916 the name was changed to Half Way House. (JHS)

This Locomobile arrived at the Mountain House in August 1900 and is believed to have been the first car to accomplish the feat. The driver is Austin Smith. It took him six hours from his home in Worcester, Massachusetts. (HCR)

The Tip Top House on the summit. It was built as a fire look-out station in 1914. (RHS)

Tip-Top House, Mt. Monadnock

The original Tip Top House was replaced in 1928 with this more substantial building. It was renovated in 1956 and until 1969 served refreshments to hikers. It was taken down in 1972. (JHS)

The summit of Pack Monadnock in Peterborough is about 1,000 feet lower than the Grand Monadnock. In 1892 the Pioneer House was built on the southwest side of the mountain. It burned a few years later and was rebuilt in a smaller version seen here about 1900. It too burned, in 1924. It was used mainly as a hunting lodge. (PHS)

It's not just Monadnock that draws hikers. The 21-mile Wapack Trail linking Mount Watatic in Ashburnham, Massachusetts, with North Pack Monadnock in Greenfield, New Hampshire, was first blazed in 1922. The Wapack Lodge was built in 1925 beside Route 124 in New Ipswich on the cellar hole of the eighteenth-century house of Deacon John Brown. For many years it offered accommodation and refreshment to hikers. Sadly, it was destroyed by fire a few years ago. (JHS)

14

Two

Village Views

Village centers tended to grow up around a community's meetinghouse: at first usually comprising a tavern, a store and a handful of houses. The towns and villages of the Monadnock region were compact and dense and remain so. Some, like Rindge, Fitzwilliam and Harrisville, developed outward from a center point, perhaps a convergence of paths, a pond, a green or a common. Others grew in a linear fashion, stretching out along the early rough roads. Dublin, shown from the north in this c. 1904 winter view, is very much of this latter pattern. Its Main Street is at least a mile in length. On the left is the Dublin Community (First Congregational) Church and just right of center is the town hall. (DHS)

Dublin village from the southwest, sometime before 1877 when the brick Trinitarian Church (above the man in the foreground), was demolished. The large building in the center is the Leffingwell Hotel, until 1908 a prominent feature in the town and one of the region's early summer hostelries. To the right of that is the Community Church. Although its heyday had passed, agriculture had certainly left its mark on the landscape: note how open and treeless the countryside was then. (DHS)

The photographer—Frank Frothingham—took this picture around 1895 from Dublin's Snow Hill. Looking northward, his grand house, which was built in 1885 by his father James and still stands, is in the center with the Farnham house behind it. (DHS)

Peterborough from East Hill about 1880. The steeples of the Baptist and Unitarian Churches are plainly visible opposite one another on Main Street. Also visible is the town house before its alteration in 1886. (PHS)

The bridge across the Minnewawa River in the foreground of this view of Marlborough is where present-day Route 124 intersects with Route 101. In the distance is the smokestack of the Valley Woolen Mill. The building on the right is the Abenaque Engine Shop which until 1941 made engines for wood sawing and hay baling. (MHS)

The building of a meetinghouse was often the first great civic activity in the early days of settlement; its construction usually mandated by the township grant. Some Monadnock region towns no longer have a meetinghouse; they may have been consumed by fire and never rebuilt. Until the 1820s the salary of the minister was paid from town taxes and the church and place for town meetings were one and same. The Toleration Act of 1819 called for the severing of connections between church and state and not long after, a church-building boom developed in the region. As churches were built the old meetinghouse typically continued on as the place for town meetings and as office space for the carrying on of town business. Sometimes, as in Jaffrey, school rooms were accommodated, and some meetinghouses continued to house both public and religious activities (still the case in Rindge and Hancock, for instance).

This 1890s view of the Jaffrey Meetinghouse was taken from Cutter's Hotel. Raised on the day of the Battle of Bunker Hill—June 17, 1775—the volunteer workers reported hearing "the far-off rumble of the guns" from Charlestown. The tower and steeple, recently refurbished, were added in 1822. (JHS)

Dublin's eye-catching town hall was built in 1882. Perhaps the citizenry tired of its "busyness" as its façade was simplified to its present appearance in 1916. Dublin's first meetinghouse was built on the Old Common—a hilltop location—but was abandoned when the center of town shifted to its present site. (DHS)

The frame of the town hall at Troy was raised on June 1, 1814. Like the meetinghouses at Hancock and Fitzwilliam, its design was influenced by the meetinghouse at Templeton, Massachusetts. Although built as the Congregational Church, today it accommodates the town offices. Troy is a newcomer as Monadnock region towns go: it was created from portions of Fitzwilliam, Marlborough, Richmond and Swanzey. (WH)

The Rindge Meetinghouse is thought to be the largest such building in northern New England. The Congregational Church still occupies the upper floor and such town functions as voting continue to take place on the first floor. Built in 1796, this is Rindge's second meetinghouse, the first being on the same site. The front was extended and a new steeple added in 1839. (RHS)

Fitzwilliam's town hall, splendidly sited on the village common, was built in 1816 as the town's second meetinghouse and church. It closely followed the design of the Templeton Meetinghouse. It burned to the ground the following year but was immediately rebuilt to the same design. Each of the four entrance columns was turned from a single pine trunk. It became the town hall in 1858. (FHS)

The Fitzwilliam Community Church at the south end of the common. Present-day Route 119 bends to the right. The church was built in 1832 by the Orthodox Society which broke away from the established church because of the "spreading creed of Unitarianism." It burned and was rebuilt in 1857. Later an additional floor was added; today the sanctuary is on the upper level, the vestry below. The house in the background was that of the Reverend John Sabin, the first pastor. (FHS)

The meetinghouse and vestry, side by side on Hancock's Main Street. Built in 1820 and, like Fitzwilliam's, attributed to Elias Carter of Templeton, Massachusetts, the meetinghouse replaced an earlier structure that burned. Originally it was situated more on the common but was moved northward to its present location in 1851. The vestry was built in 1836 as the Hancock Academy. Congregational Church services are held on the second floor of the meeting house and up until 1985 the first floor was the site of the annual town meeting. Like its counterpart in Jaffrey, the splendid steeple was recently removed, restored and re-installed. A curving row of horse sheds behind the meetinghouse replaced those visible on the left in 1895. (HHS)

Marlborough's town hall incorporated retail space on the ground floor and the Grange on the top floor. The selectmen's office was on the second floor; the town jail and "hobo quarters" in the basement. It burned in 1961 and was replaced two years later by the present town offices and fire and police stations. (MHS)

An archetypal New England village scene, sometime before 1882. The Harrisville Canal is in the foreground, the handsome Greek revival Evangelical Congregational Church, built in 1842, is on the right and the brick vestry, originally a chapel and now the town library, is on the left. (JHS)

Dublin's shingle-style Emmanuel Church was built in 1888, the cost being largely borne by summer residents. Mary and Margaret Greene donated $2,000 in memory of their sister, Mrs. Caspar Crowninshield. The building itself has not changed at all over the years. (DHS)

Peterborough's first meetinghouse on this site (Grove and Main Streets) was built in 1860. It was altered almost beyond recognition in 1886. When it was heavily damaged by fire in 1916, the decision was made to rebuild but to a new design. This photograph is dated December 9, 1916, as demolition began. (PHS)

By the end of March in 1917, the site had been cleared awaiting the construction of the new town house. Virtually all the buildings in the background are now gone. The large structure on the hilltop is the old Central School. (PHS)

The present town house nearing completion. The architect was B.F.W. Russell; the cost, $68,000. The first town meeting held in the new building was on March 12, 1918. (PHS)

The First Baptist Church on Main Street, decked out with bunting for Peterborough's Old Home Day of 1902. The church, still an important downtown landmark, was dedicated in 1842. It has always had shops on the ground floor. The railroad depot can be made out in the distance on the left. (PHS)

Dublin's Community (First Congregational) Church, built in 1852, suffered in a bizarre manner on September 21, 1938 when the steeple plunged through the roof at the height of the great hurricane. (DHS)

This view is of the second floor sanctuary showing the top section of the surprisingly intact steeple. It was rebuilt from scratch and re-installed. (DHS)

Not unlike meetinghouses, some Monadnock region towns are fortunate enough to still have a fine common or green as a community focal point. This view is of Fitzwilliam's. Others—Dublin and Peterborough, for instance—had commons early on but abandoned them when the town centers shifted, often from a hilltop to better protected lower ground. Town commons were public open space, used for gathering, military training and livestock grazing. Visible at the rear in this c. 1890s view is, on the left, what is now the Fitzwilliam Inn. In the center is the Fitzwilliam Hotel—now gone—and to the right the Parker store. The local granite quarries probably supplied the fence posts that help define Fitzwilliam's common. (FHS)

Another view of the Fitzwilliam Common, this time looking south. In the center is the Civil War Monument, dedicated in 1871. The Fairbanks scale in the foreground is long gone; it was used to weigh livestock and wagons. Similar scales at Rindge and Temple happily survive. Granite signposts are still found here and there throughout the region; they seem to convey more information than their modern counterparts. (FHS)

A view of the Troy Common, sometime before 1882. It was probably photographed from atop the town hall. In 1941, when the state widened the road, the common was greatly altered and the granite and wood fence was removed (the granite posts were buried in two holes on the common). Just recently the fence was re-installed. (JHS)

Looking south from the steeple of the Hancock Meetinghouse. On the far side of the somewhat woebegone common is the Turner Building, built in 1836 by the Baptists as the Literary and Scientific Institute. In the 1890s—about the date of this view— it was shifted slightly and renovated for use as Schoolhouse No. 1. It still serves as a town school. (HHS)

The West Rindge Common looking westward. The watering trough, a feature often associated with the town common, is still in the same location. The Methodist Church in the distance was built in 1835 and moved to this location—it stands just off Route 202—in 1882. The railroad line ran behind where the photographer stood. (RHS)

Throughout the Monadnock region, as elsewhere in New England, Main Street was what tied the community together and gave it its identity: along it stretched the shops, residences, institutions and industries that were the heart of the town. But it also linked each town to the next. Beyond Main Street lay the farms and forests. Today, a century later, there are far fewer of the former and considerably more of the latter.

This view of Main Street, Marlborough, dates from around the turn of the century. The Universalist Church on the left came down in the early 1960s. Originally a single story, it was raised up so that a vestry could be built below. The steeple of the Methodist Church pokes up on the right. The building survives as the Community House, but the steeple itself was lost in the fire of 1933. (MHS)

Hancock's Main Street with the meetinghouse and the Hancock Inn in the distance. By the 1920s, once the automobile had established itself, most Monadnock towns paved their major roads. A memorable aspect of Hancock's present streetscape is its fences, an example of which, still extant, can be seen on the right. Unlike most of its neighbors, the village still retains its narrow, somewhat meandering gravel footpaths. (HHS)

The north side of Hancock's Main Street, sometime after 1894. Flanking Fred Eaton's store, which served as the post office between 1897 and 1902, are the Hancock Inn on the left and the Whitcomb Town Library on the right. The library, completed in 1882, was enlarged and altered almost beyond recognition in 1925. A rear extension was added in the 1980s. Route 202 bypassed the village in 1959 doing much to preserve one of the region's most attractive Main Streets. (HHS)

Looking toward the Troy Common with the Stone Bridge in the foreground. The roadway is now Route 12. The bandstand can just be made out on the common, on the far side of which stands the Monadnock Hotel. To the right, just out of the picture, was the original Troy Blanket Mill. The superintendent, Barrett Ripley, lived in the house on the left. (WH)

View to the south from an upper window of the Fitzwilliam Hotel. The corner building was built in 1837; in later years it was the residence and law office of Amos J. Blake. It is now the home of the Fitzwilliam Historical Society. (FHS)

A westward view along Dublin's Main Street (Route 101), no later than 1900. To the left are Gleason's store and the town hall with its distinctive curving canopy and beyond that, the Leffingwell Hotel. On the right is the Mason store, and on the hill, the Willcox Inn. The building in between is now part of the offices of *Yankee Magazine*. It would be years before Main Street would be paved. Without much in the way of street trees the village must have been hot and dusty during summer dry spells. (DHS)

Fences are an important ingredient in the charm of any New England village. This picturesque view along King Road in New Ipswich is toward Main Street. The Homestead Inn, which burned in 1929, is on the right. Part of the Grange on Main Street can be seen on the far right. (NIHS)

Main Street, New Ipswich, at the Turnpike (Route 124) intersection. The building on the left was the Corner Store and post office; it is now a parking lot. The watering fountain was installed in 1893: it had a low trough for dogs, a higher one for horses and a bubbler for humans. It also had a built-in street light. (NIHS)

Looking eastward in Fitzwilliam along what is now Route 119, *c.* 1894. The common is on the right and the Fitzwilliam Hotel and the village store on the left. Note the hay wagon in the distance. (FHS)

This handsome building in Fitzwilliam is Schoolhouse No. 5, built in 1823. It still stands today on the Upper Troy Road, without its steeple and now converted to a residence. This group photograph dates from 1898. (FHS)

Looking down Peterborough's Grove Street with Main Street in the foreground. The town house appears on the right prior to its dramatic facelift in 1886. On the opposite corner is what is now referred to as the Granite Block. When this view was taken (pre-1876) Ebenezer Jones ran the clothing store; later it was run by A.B. Tarbell (who owned the building) and then by John Wilder. Two floors were added to the building following the 1902 fire. (PHS)

Main Street, Peterborough. One Pine, a housing complex, has since been developed in the foreground. In the distance on the right is the library; the entrance portico was added in 1914. The Unitarian Church steeple is in the center with the old Central School on the hilltop in the distance. The buildings on the left were destroyed in the fire that followed the 1938 hurricane. (PHS)

The present Peterborough Library was built in 1893 although the library itself was founded in 1833. It is generally accepted to have been the first free public library in America, although this claim has been challenged even by neighboring Dublin! Originally the collection was in the Smith & Thompson's store and then for many years in the basement of the town house. It was designed by George S. Morison. (PHS)

The interior of the Peterborough Library, probably shortly after it opened. (PHS)

This 1953 photograph is of Mary Bemis, the postmistress at Chesham in Harrisville. The post office remains a community focus throughout the region but in days past it was even more central to everyday life. Besides a place to send and receive mail, it was a social center, a place for learning the latest news and in most cases a place to buy groceries and the other necessities of life. Few post offices are still carried on as adjuncts to the village store. Today's trend toward ever-larger regional stores and shopping malls has made the small general store a threatened species. (HHI)

Goodnow's store in Jaffrey with Charles Letourneau driving the delivery wagon. Goodnow's became very successful and expanded to other towns: at its height there were twenty-three stores throughout the region and in other New England states. The Jaffrey store closed in 1967 and was replaced by the parking lot of the Monadnock Bank. (JHS)

The interior of Goodnow's in its heyday. Most Monadnock region towns had a comparable store where you could get nearly everything you really needed. (JHS)

Main Street in Hancock. Farmer's store is on the left. It was built in 1878 and continues in business, somewhat enlarged, as the Hancock Market. The post office was here between 1886 and 1890 and again between 1893 and 1897. Its location would alternate between the two stores in the village depending on which party was in power in Washington. (HHS)

C.W. Farmer sold his Hancock store to Will Fogg, seen here in the doorway, in 1896. Will Hayward is in the delivery wagon. The Foggs ran the store until 1926. (HHS)

M.D. Mason's store in Dublin. The original portion of the store was built in 1840; the front section was added in 1869. The building is still standing but the store closed in the early 1980s. Beside it is the Mason cottage which was incorporated into the offices of *Yankee Magazine*. (DHS)

Across Dublin's Main Street from the Mason store was Gleason's. It was replaced by another building in 1966. The town's first telephone exchange was on the second floor. (DHS)

This Main Street structure was built in 1843 as the Marlborough Hotel and became well known as a temperance hotel. When this photograph was taken, Goodnow Bemis Co. (clothing and novelties) and Adams & Atwood (groceries) had shop space on the ground floor. The hotel and the connected Lawrence Livery Stables burned in 1970. The site today is occupied by Doody's Mini Mart. (MHS)

This shop interior in Marlborough is probably that of Adams & Atwood. (MHS)

The old Wilder store in Rindge Center. Built around 1790 and located close to the common, it was destroyed by fire. (RHS)

The Fuller store, also in Rindge Center. It continues in business opposite the meetinghouse as the Village Grocer. E.A. Fuller is on the far right. (RHS)

This photograph dates to about 1871 and shows the Parker store, opposite the common in Fitzwilliam. It was built in 1859 and continues in business today as the Fitzwilliam Common Market. (FHS)

For many years the Thayer Cigar Factory was the largest employer in New Ipswich. Its cigars were sold throughout the country. Sometime in the 1930s the building was converted to a grocery; it is now the New Ipswich Market. (NIHS)

This view of Collins' store on Marlborough's Main Street dates to 1891. Collins' was a small-scale department store of the sort sorely missed by all. Later the building was used as the American Legion Hall; today it is a pizza parlor. As with many Marlborough buildings good use of the town's quarried granite was made in its construction. (MHS)

Next to Collins' was B.F. Merriam's stove and tinware shop. The Merriam family—B.F. is at the far left—and a helper are pictured in this mid-1880s view. The Main Street building still stands and is now the Hall & Croteau Funeral Chapel. (MHS)

The interior of the Nationwide Grocery in Harrisville which was located in the brick Harris Storehouse, the present weaving center of Harrisville Designs. This photograph probably dates to sometime in the 1930s. Pictured behind the counter are John and Bernice Clark, the proprietors. During this era chain stores such as the First National and A & P were making great inroads in the Monadnock region. (HHI)

Pictured inside Belletete's store on North Street in Jaffrey are Emile Labrie and Elie Belletete. The building still stands but the business relocated to Peterborough Street in 1958 where it remains today, although now dealing only in hardware and building supplies. (JHS)

The Winch & Field store on Grove Street in Peterborough. Originally it was the Union Store and later Lloyd's, the Peterborough Cash Market and the Monadnock Shop. Today it is the Winged Pig. Note the delivery wagons; the shoe factory looms in the distance. (PHS)

The First National in Peterborough was located on lower Main Street in what is now known as the Centertown building. Between two second floor windows is the shingle of Perkins Bass. The former congressman (1954–62) moved his law offices to the Peterborough Historical Society building in 1952 and they remain there today. (PHS)

Derby's was a Peterborough mainstay on Grove Street for many years. This 1908 view shows Horace Bevis and Johnny Allen on their delivery wagons. The building surivives but Derby's closed a few years ago. The tenant is now Peterborough Furniture. (PHS)

The staff of Derby's on July 10, 1942, the sixtieth anniversary of the business. The many different shop fronts of Derby's over the years document well the changes in taste and fashion in American retailing. (PHS)

48

The second floor interior of Derby's in 1912. (PHS)

The lunch cart in Jaffrey near the Peterborough Street and Main Street intersection. The tower of the Jaffrey Mills can be seen at the rear left. This version of the tower replaced the original around 1897. Lunch carts and later, diners, were first developed in New England and proved very popular. This cart was moved more than once within the downtown area. (JHS)

Along with meetinghouses and post offices, the inn or hotel was always an important landmark in a town. Offering more than food and lodging, it was typically a venue for social and fraternal gatherings and often included shops and other services such as a livery stable. During the days of stage travel inns were hives of activity once the coach arrived. Some were able to capitalize successfully on the coming of the railroad, especially when summer boarders began to visit the region to escape the heat of the city. With the advent of automobile travel, however, many of these same hostelries found survival difficult.

Such was the case with The Tavern in Peterborough. Established sometime in the 1830s, the Main Street hotel was called French's until 1879 when the Tucker family purchased it. When this photograph was taken it was called Tucker's Hotel, though it was later renamed The Tavern. The premises included a variety of shops; note the signboard of George Scripture, a pioneering Peterborough photographer, who had his studio here. The Tavern was demolished in 1965 to be replaced by the Peterborough Savings Bank building. All that remains today to remind one of the hotel is the massive granite pillar, visible to the left, that is now the bank's signpost. (PHS)

The lobby of The Tavern not long before the building was torn down. (WH)

The Hancock Inn was built in 1789 and has been a feature of Hancock life since then. It has gone by a number of names in its long history: Fox Tavern, Jefferson Tavern, Hancock Hotel, Hancock House and John Hancock Inn. The business was started by Noah Wheeler; other memorable innkeepers were David "Squire" Patten and John Eaton. Eaton added the ell and the third story sometime after 1875. (HHS)

For many years Fitzwilliam's two best-known hotels stood across the street from one another. This view from the common, with the 1871 Civil War Monument in the foreground, shows the Cheshire Hotel on the left and the Fitzwilliam Hotel on the right. The former dates from 1793 although the present building was probably erected around 1843. Its earlier name was the Goldsmith Tavern. In 1973 the Cheshire was renamed the Fitzwilliam Inn. The Fitzwilliam Hotel, on the right, was built in 1807. In the 1830s it was operated as Columbia House and in 1870s as Gage's Hotel. It was taken down in 1946, and its site is still vacant. (FHS)

Summer boarders at the Fitzwilliam Hotel sometime in the 1890s. The building no longer stands. (FHS)

Summer porch-sitting across the street at the Cheshire Hotel. It is now called the Fitzwilliam Inn and is still a popular destination in summer and winter. (FHS)

One of largest and best-known taverns built to serve travelers on the Third New Hampshire Turnpike was Prescott's Inn, a large brick Federal-style building that opened in 1803 in Jaffrey. It was torn down in 1948 although its Rufus Porter mural was saved and installed in the lobby of a Boston hotel. (JHS)

The front doorway of Prescott's Inn probably shortly before its demolition. The site, an overgrown field, is opposite the Millipore factory on Route 124. (JHS)

The original Shattuck Inn on Jaffrey's Dublin Road. Built in 1806, the house was expanded to accommodate the growing number of summer boarders that Mrs. Shattuck began to take in around 1868. Once the railroad became established in the 1870s, catering to summer visitors became an increasingly important part of the regional economy. (JHS)

The Shattuck burned to the ground in 1909, but a new and far larger building was ready for business by July of the following year. Willa Cather was the new inn's most famous regular guest. The building stands vacant and has not operated as an inn for many years. (JHS)

Clark's Hotel or the 1808 House in New Ipswich. This was an important inn on the Third New Hampshire Turnpike; the two-day mail stage journey between Boston and Walpole was broken in New Ipswich. It was one of three taverns in the town along the turnpike and the only one that still stands today, although it is no longer an inn. Joseph Silver owned it between 1892 and 1910. He and his family are pictured here. (NIHS)

The Marlborough Hotel, not to be confused by another of the same name on the other side of Main Street, was run by Ray Tarbox when this photograph was taken in 1929. It was built much earlier, in 1792, and was originally called the Old Red Tavern. It operated as a hotel until 1930 and was later replaced by a gas station. (MHS)

John Cutter, a prominent person in early Jaffrey history, built this large house in 1790. Like many others in the region, the family took in summer boarders beginning in the mid-1800s. It went by a variety of names: in this c. 1880 stereoscopic view it is called the Central House. At other times it was operated as Rice's Hotel and briefly as the Shattuck House while the Shattuck Inn was being rebuilt. The back ell has been shortened and much of the porch removed and once again it is a private residence. (JHS)

This was Jaffrey's third Granite State Hotel, the previous two having burned. This, the last in the line, also succumbed to fire in 1923. It was located where the present town offices stand. The building to the right still exists. The Granite State Hotel was the center of activity in what was then called East Jaffrey. (JHS)

The Monadnock Hotel, on the west side of the Troy Common, about 1910. It was built by Josiah Morse in 1802. The portion in the foreground was taken down in the early 1940s and is now a parking lot. The ell to the left remains although much changed. (WH)

This large building on the south side of Dublin's Main Street started out as the residence of Joseph Appleton. For a while it was run as a hotel called the Appleton House. Dr. C.H. Leffingwell purchased it in 1871 and over the years expanded it often to accommodate the growing number of summer visitors. For many years the Leffingwell, as it was known, was the only hotel in town. This photograph dates to the summer of 1886. The Leffingwell was destroyed by fire in November 1908. (DHS)

This grand Dublin twenty-seven-room cottage was built in 1880 by E.H. Hamilton in the vicinity of the present-day Dublin School. Between 1910 and 1914 it was run as a summer hotel and called the Willcox Inn. It was demolished around 1936. (DHS)

Cutter's Hotel stood close to the Jaffrey Meetinghouse. Established in 1792, it burned in 1816, was rebuilt in brick as seen here, and then burned again in 1901. It was sited where the flagpole now stands within a few feet of Main Street. It was particularly prosperous when the Third New Hampshire Turnpike was active and later in the century when the summer visitor trade flourished. (JHS)

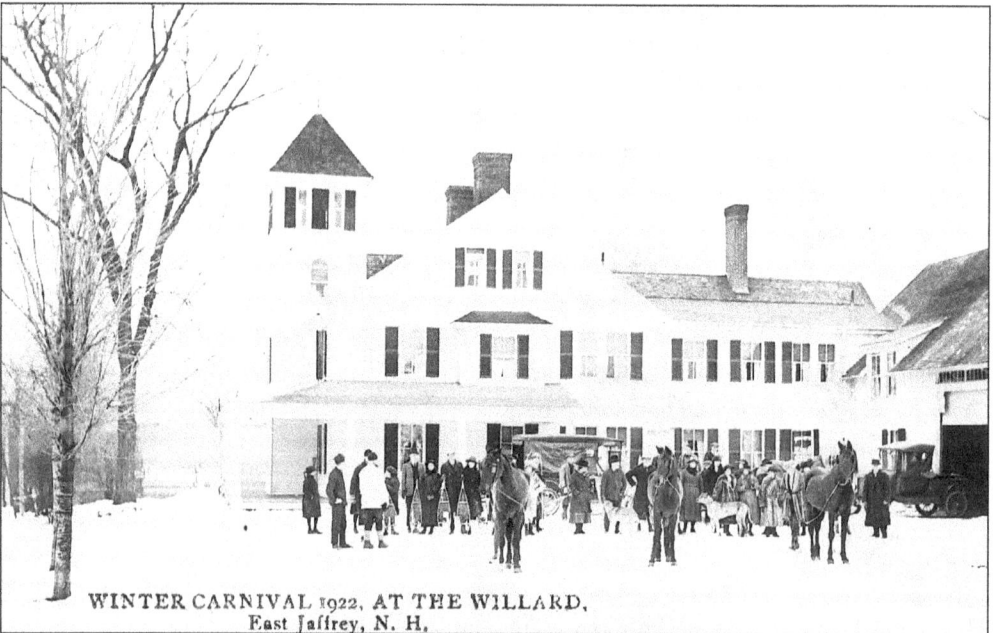

WINTER CARNIVAL 1922, AT THE WILLARD,
East Jaffrey, N. H.

The Willard Hotel on Jaffrey's Stratton Road. It is no longer a hotel but in the 1920s it was a popular place, as seen here during the Jaffrey Winter Carnival. (JHS)

Three

Work: Farming, Forestry, Quarrying and Mills

Agriculture was the dominant economic activity in the Monadnock region until the coming of the mills and later the railroad. Even as late as the early part of the present century, open fields and hillsides were the rule and woodland the exception. This old stereoscopic view shows hand haying in Jaffrey Center in 1869. The stooping figure is Nathaniel Cutter; the standing man, the Reverend Henry Shedd. The Cutter Cemetery can be seen in the rear and in the distance the long ell of the John Cutter house, still standing. Jaffrey Center lies just beyond with Mount Monadnock in the distance. (JHS)

By far the most remarkable farm complex in the region was Jones Wilder's Cheshire Place, a 7,000-acre, self-contained farming community in Rindge, developed over twelve years beginning in 1882. The farmworkers numbered 150; there were 500 cattle and 200 horses. The large and beautifully laid stone walls pictured here can still be seen. (RHS)

Wilder's thirty-room house at Cheshire Place. Reduced in size and remodeled in 1925, it is now the main building of the Hampshire Country School which occupies some of the original 7,000 acres. (RHS)

The three important New Hampshire centers of granite quarrying were Concord, Milford and Fitzwilliam. The former two still have active quarries but the Fitzwilliam operation has long been dormant. This marvelous example of stone carving was a product of the Webb Hill Quarry in Fitzwilliam. Where it is today is a mystery but it may have been intended as a cemetery monument for some now-forgotten lumber baron. Fitzwilliam granite was known for its fine grain and lightness of color. In 1886, the town shipped 7,080 tons of granite to destinations throughout the Northeast. The peak of the industry was around 1915 when three hundred workers were employed, mostly Italians and Finns. A railroad spur track was built from the quarry to Fitzwilliam Depot around which finishing yards were operated. (FHS)

The George O. King Granite Works, a finishing shed near the depot in Fitzwilliam. Fitzwilliam granite was often elaborately carved for the architectural trim of buildings in Boston, Worcester, New York and other East Coast cities. (FHS)

Charles Reed was the first to quarry in Fitzwilliam on a commercial scale. He set up his business in 1864. By the time of this photograph his son, Daniel, was heading the operation. It was absorbed by Webb's in 1882. (FHS)

The steam traction engine used for hauling granite along the spur track from the quarry to Fitzwilliam Depot. (FHS)

Blast at Webb's Quarry, June 30, 1896.

Marlborough was a granite quarrying center as well. Webb's Quarry is in the southwest corner of the town and was connected by rail to Webb Depot on the line to Keene. The operation was started by Asa Greenwood in 1831. George Webb bought it in 1891. (MHS)

Webb & Batchelder's Quarry in Marlborough. The quarry was closed in 1934; activity had been declining since 1914 when George Webb died in a railroad accident. (MHS)

Although weighing several tons this large block of Marlborough granite does not seem to strain the wagon in the least. (MHS)

Elwin Jewell's stable in West Rindge. Much of his business was carried on in the woods, hauling logs. Rindge, Jaffrey and Marlborough have had many enterprises, large and small, tied to forest products: boxes, turnings, baskets, toys, clothespins, matches and sawed lumber. (RHS)

Another Rindge business tied to the woods: The Union Box and Lumber Co. in East Rindge. In 1885 it was cutting 2,000 cords of wood per year for use in the manufacture of small wood boxes. The company operated until about 1935. The building was used for a time to make skis and was finally destroyed by fire in the 1940s. (RHS)

The Whitney Brothers mill in Marlborough manufactured wooden toys. Shown here in 1901 is the workforce; perhaps the man by the massive granite watering trough is one of the Whitneys. This building burned, was rebuilt, and burned again in 1933. It was on Route 101 about a mile east of the center of town. (MHS)

Julius Bemis's smithy in Fitzwilliam around 1907. The smith is seen on the right with his dog. The rear of the town hall can be seen on the far left. The building was taken down in the 1920s and the site remains vacant. In the days when farming and the horse held sway, every town had at least one blacksmith; often several. (FHS)

68

In the early days of the settlement of the Monadnock region, in the second half of the eighteenth century and really up to the mid-nineteenth century, industry was small and mostly a natural outgrowth of the reigning economy: agriculture and forestry. Saw and grist mills were common; so too tanneries, potash burning and maple sugaring. This was to change with the introduction of the textile industry to New Hampshire in 1808 when the first mill was put into operation in New Ipswich. The development of mills was rapid throughout the region: Peterborough, Troy, Marlborough and Jaffrey soon were humming with industrial activity. The upper mill at Harrisville, once the northern section of Dublin, was built in the early 1830s. Other mill buildings followed. The Lower or Stone Mill pictured here was built about 1848 and the adjoining brick addition to the right a few years later. The entire village is a National Historic Landmark, the country's only almost intact nineteenth-century industrial community. (HHI)

Peterborough's Phoenix Mill was built in 1828 after a fire destroyed its predecessor. The site was behind the present Peterborough Historical Society building. Much of today's downtown was at one time owned by the mill. The town house was, in fact, built on Phoenix Mill land. The graceful twin-towered mill was torn down in 1922. (PHS)

Noone's Mills were among the first in Peterborough, established in 1813 for wool carding. They were twice destroyed by fire. The cupola came down in the 1938 hurricane. In 1980 the mills ceased textile production but continue as an attractive retail complex. (PHS)

Thomas Goodall, from Yorkshire, England, came to Troy in 1851 and a few years later started a blanket mill, the first in America to produce blankets designed specifically for horses. In 1865 he sold out to a partnership which carried on the business as the Troy Blanket Mills. One of the partners, Barrett Ripley, became the superintendent, the first of five generations of Ripleys linked with what is now called simply Troy Mills. In 1910 the mills turned out 1,200 horse blankets and 2,000 yards of coat lining each day. In recent years the specialty has been non-woven trim for the automobile industry. This view shows the new brick mill which was built in 1869 and expanded in 1877 and 1880. Expansion of the complex continues today. (WH)

The Jaffrey Mills were built in stages beginning in 1868 on a site beside the Contoocook River. The brick complex, listed on the National Register of Historic Places, is still very much a landmark in the center of downtown Jaffrey. Main Street is in the foreground. The original town bandstand can be seen on the common only a few feet from where the present one stands. The towering Town Elm finally succumbed in 1934. The mill's original graceful cupola was replaced with one of a different design, probably in 1897 when an addition along North Street was built. Although the complex is occupied by a variety of businesses, textile production is a thing of the past. This view dates from about 1880. (JHS)

The interior of the Jaffrey Mills sometime after 1897, when a major addition was built. Cotton textiles, particularly denim, were the main products. (JHS)

Another view in the Jaffrey Mills. Except for the absence of the machinery the interior is mostly unchanged and is easily recognizable today. (JHS)

The substantial High Bridge Mill in New Ipswich was built about 1875. It still stands although alterations have stripped it of much of its original elegance. The intricate gable brickwork seen in this view is also visible from Route 124. (NIHS)

Felt's Machine Shop on Elm Street in Peterborough. The company manufactured textile and wood-working machinery and later suction pumps. Built on the site of the old Eagle Factory, the building pictured here burned in 1875. In 1893 a new three-story shop was built by H.B. Needham as a basket factory which it remained until the business relocated in 1906 to a site behind the Baptist Church. Later it became the Goyette Museum. (PHS)

Lower Main Street, Peterborough, with the Baptist Church on the right, the Davis Block on the left and what started off in 1884 as a shoe factory on Depot Street in the center. By 1895 the New York Piano-Forte Key Co. had replaced shoemaking and eleven years later the Needham Basket Company moved in. Note the barber pole in front of the Davis Block. Roy's Market now stands at this corner. (PHS)

Baskets are still produced in Peterborough. This extra large one was made by the Needham Basket Company sometime after 1906 when the business moved into the former piano factory on Depot Street. (PHS)

The "New Mill" at Harrisville, built in 1867. It only stood for fifteen years, burning in 1882 under somewhat suspicious circumstances. This photograph shows the mill before a mansard roof was added to the tower. (JHS)

Barbara McGiness in front of a Jacquard loom thought to be in the New Mill in Harrisville, probably in the 1870s. Power loom weaving ceased at Harrisville in 1970 but handweaving continues, as does the manufacture and sale of weaving looms and supplies by Harrisville Designs, a business carried on by the descendants of the Colony family who owned the mills from the mid-1880s onwards. (HHI)

The Monadnock Blanket Mill in Marlborough was established in 1868. This 1910 view is looking toward the northwest; South Main Street is just out of the picture to the left. The mill produced horse blankets, finally closing about 1953. It was torn down around 1963 but the mill bell now hangs in the new bell tower beside Route 101 close to the original mill site. (MHS)

Warren H. Clark in his office at the Valley Woolen Mill in Marlborough. Established in 1869 as a chair mill, it shifted to producing horse blankets when Clark entered into a partnership with Charles O. Whitney in 1873 under the name Cheshire Blanket Mill. In 1913 the name was changed to Valley Woolen Mill. The Route 101 site is today occupied by the Wilber Brothers Market. (MHS)

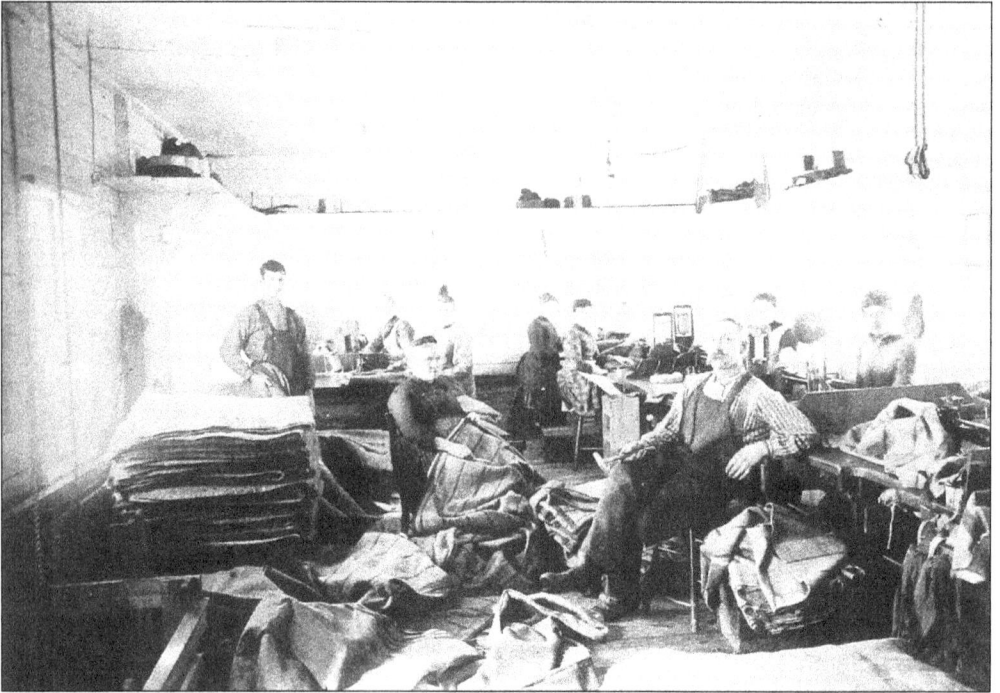

Interior of the Valley Woolen Mill in Marlborough. Horse blankets were the chief product. (MHS)

Another interior scene at the Valley Woolen Mill. Between 1939 and 1952 the mill was operated as the Medford-Marlborough Knit Garter Co. (MHS)

Four

Leisure: Sports, Outings, Dramatic Doings, Town Bands and Parades

Leisure-time activities, sports and recreation have always been a part of life in the Monadnock region, although what is popular today was often unknown in years past. Without television, movies and the mobility offered by the automobile and airplane, our predecessors were more apt to rely on one another when spending their time away from work and school. And for the most part they did so locally. Fishing and hunting were and remain popular. Dramatics and outings and climbing the mountain also continue to draw enthusiasts. Years ago nearly every town had a band of some description; they marched in parades, performed in the bandstand on the common on summer evenings or supplied the music at dances. Boys and men in every town also played baseball, perhaps for their school or club or, as pictured here, on a company-sponsored team. Jaffrey's "Tack" shop—now W.W. Cross—was at the time of this photograph the town's largest employer. Klean-Kutt was one of the company's trade names. (JHS)

The Appleton Base Ball Club of New Ipswich posing in front of Clark's Hotel about 1880. (NIHS)

This undated and unlabeled photograph is of the Peterborough High School team, judging from the uniforms. (PHS)

A group of well-dressed ballplayers on what may be the steps of the Rindge Schoolhouse early in this century. (RHS)

A Jaffrey ball team arranged in ascending order, probably in the early 1920s. (JHS)

Marlborough bicyclists in front of the schoolhouse fence. The sport was very much in vogue around 1900 when this photograph was probably taken. Shown are Nettie Whitney Richardson, Florence Whitney and an unidentified friend. (MHS)

A party of cyclists in front of Charles Taylor's house in Smith Village, New Ipswich, in 1898. (NIHS)

Fishing has always been a relaxing summer diversion as demonstrated by these young Harrisville anglers trying their luck in Chesham. (HHI)

Thaddeus and John Morse, father and son, fishing at the outlet of Dublin Lake, probably in the late 1870s. The Morses were a large Dublin family stretching over several generations. The town history refers to Captain Thomas Morse as Dublin's first permanent English settler. (DHS)

A pleasant summer scene at the Barr house in New Ipswich around the turn of the century. Pictured are the Misses Caroline Barr and Mary Barrett and, standing, possibly Elizabeth Barr Keyser. (NIHS)

Formality of dress didn't seem to inhibit these croquet players on the Fitzwilliam Common sometime prior to 1871. The trees are now stately veterans. (FHS)

An obviously lively group from the Murdock School on an outing to Contoocook Lake about 1900. (JHS)

The Marlborough Business Men's picnic at Tolman Pond in nearby Nelson on September 2, 1901. Given the occasion, they appear overly glum. (MHS)

A gathering of the Jowders family at its camp on Contoocook Lake in 1893. When Red Dam was built in Jaffrey, the lake increased in size and depth making it ripe for development. Further encouragement came when the railroad pushed north from Winchendon and a small station—Woodmere—was built beside the lake. The Jowders, from New Ipswich, built three cottages at the south end of the lake in the 1880s and soon after a summer colony grew up around them. (RHS)

For close to fifty years, summer plays were presented, largely for the fun of it, at "Loon Point," the property of Joseph Lindon Smith on the south side of Dublin Lake. The date of this production is not known. (DHS)

This play was staged in 1939 for George Markham's birthday. It was held at "Teatro Bambino," one of two outdoor theatres at "Loon Point." (DHS)

Close to Dublin Lake is Dark Pond. Outdoor plays were held here as well, in a rustic amphitheatre. In 1934 a production was staged to honor Amelia Earhart, who had Dublin relatives. The famous aviatrix is in the back row surrounded by young cast members, several of whom still live nearby. (DHS)

Dublin wasn't the only town in the region prone to theatrical extravaganzas. Peterborough's Out-Door Players—two cast members of which are pictured here—was launched in 1912 by Marie Ware Laughton at a sylvan setting on the Middle Hancock Road. Summer plays were presented for many years. Peterborough could also boast Mariarden and, today, the Peterborough Players. (PHS)

These young girls sold souvenirs at the Jaffrey sesquicentennial celebration held between August 11th and 18th, 1923. The week was filled with parades, bonfires, speeches, debates, a ball game, a gymkhana on the old parade ground, teas and—as the town history records—"marvellous real Jaffrey weather." (VIS)

"An Old Fashioned Lyceum" held at Melville Academy as one of the many Jaffrey sesquicentennial events. At the far right is Mrs. Margaret Robinson, president of the Village Improvement Society for twenty years and the major force in the 1922 restoration of the Jaffrey Meetinghouse. Seventy years later another major restoration effort was taken on by the citizens of Jaffrey, demonstrating the same spirit and pride in their town's heritage. Melville Academy continues today as a restored schoolhouse and local history museum. (VIS)

Town bands were all the rage for many years. They sprang up following the Civil War, probably as a natural accompaniment to the many GAR patriotic parades and memorial dedications. There was a social element about them, and no doubt avid competition arose between the towns when it came to repertoire, marching and musical skill and the extravagance of uniforms. It wasn't uncommon for town appropriations to be made for the purchase of instruments. In Jaffrey, stock was even sold for this purpose at $10.00 a share; in 1875 a dividend of $2.20 was actually paid out to shareholders! Town bands inevitably led to bandstands, many of which still stand—and are still used—around the region. In 1986, Jaffrey's bandstand was moved back to the common and restored.

The Hancock Cornet Band appears to be well turned out in this 1908 photograph. The members are assembled in front of the vestry on Main Street. As is usually the case, the drum major is the tallest bandmember. (HHS)

Hornplayer Albert L. Howe was for thirty years a member of both the New Ipswich and neighboring Ashby bands. (NIHS)

The New Ipswich Band around 1900. Albert Howe may be the gentleman with the moustache right of center. (NIHS)

The East Jaffrey Cornet Band about 1885. The band's first performance was on May 11, 1873. Behind the bandmembers, who are fashionably equipped with handsome headwear, stands the Granite State Hotel (the site of the present town offices) and beyond, the original stair tower and cupola of the Jaffrey Mills. (JHS)

The East Jaffrey Cornet Band twenty-three years later, in 1908, marching east on Main Street. The Mower or Riverside Block, in the background, burned down in 1927. (JHS)

The Fitzwilliam Brass Band on an excursion to Ashby, Massachusetts, on September 30, 1887. That town's meetinghouse is the backdrop. (FHS)

The Rindge Cornet Band also traveled to other towns in the region. Here it is photographed on Fair Day in front of the Fitzwilliam Town Hall in 1918. (RHS)

The Peterborough Cornet Band in 1866. Behind is the town house twenty years before its facelift. The Tarbell building on the left was severely damaged by fire in 1902; when rebuilt, an additional two floors were added. Today, referred to as the Granite Block, it is home to more than one award-winning architect. The influence of the Civil War can be seen in the uniforms; some of the bandmembers may even have served in that conflict. The large drum is now in the collection of the Peterborough Historical Society. (PHS)

The Peterborough Cadet Band lined up in front of the Unitarian Church on Main Street in 1889. The drum major, not being quite the tallest, needs some help from a plumed helmet. The band was participating in the town's one hundred and fiftieth anniversary celebration. (PHS)

Bands didn't always march, as can be seen here on the shores of Contoocook Lake in Rindge. The setting is the spiritualist campground that was developed in 1884 for religious camp meetings. Back then, Contoocook was called Lake Sunshine. (RHS)

The Contoocook Singing Orchestra of East Jaffrey. The leader and cornetist was Alfred L. Towne. Beginning in 1903 the band, composed mostly of family members, performed several times a week at gatherings throughout the region. It disbanded in 1932. (JHS)

Parades, like bands, were and are important events in the annual calendar of Monadnock region towns. This is a view looking westward of Peterborough's 1903 Memorial Day parade. The procession is probably headed out Concord Street to the Village and Pine Hill Cemeteries. (PHS)

The Fourth of July parade in Jaffrey in 1911. The procession is moving along Peterborough Street with Main Street in the left background. Since 1941 the Dillon Block has occupied the corner behind the float. Notice the rail car that is on the spur track that served the Jaffrey Mills. (JHS)

A float in Jaffrey's sesquicentennial parade on August 17, 1923. The replica, built by Albert E. Knight, commemorates the town's first schoolhouse, very similar to the restored Little Red Schoolhouse which stands today beside the meetinghouse in Jaffrey Center. (JHS)

Jaffrey's sesquicentennial celebration was a week-long affair. The parade was undoubtedly the highlight event. World War I having ended not long before, this contingent is probably made up of veterans; over one hundred Jaffrey men served their country in the conflict. (JHS)

The Ashby Band and the GAR contingent marching along what is now Route 124 in New Ipswich on Memorial Day, probably in the 1880s. They may be headed to the Soldiers' Monument. (NIHS)

Very likely this is the same parade as above, here assembled on Appleton Common at the Soldiers' Monument which was dedicated in 1878. (NIHS)

Memorial Day ceremonies at Harrisville in 1946, the first held after the conclusion of World War II. Abel Twitchell's house, around which Harrisville developed, can just be made out in the far right background. (HHI)

Dublin's bicentennial parade in 1952. Dressed in period costumes are Henry Gowing and his sister Alice, descendants of Henry Strongman, the first permanent resident. Most Monadnock region towns have more than one claimant to the title of first settler. In Dublin, Colonel William Thornton and Thomas Morse are also among those so honored. (DHS)

Five

Fire and Flood

Fires and floods and other disasters are often imprinted on the community mind well past the lifespans of those who experienced them firsthand. The year with no summer—1816—when frost was recorded in every month and few crops survived is still remarked upon throughout New England. In this century the great hurricane of September 1938 is a common topic of conversation. The effect it had on Monadnock region towns was monumental, in the destruction of property, loss of life and the change it wrought to the landscape of both town and countryside. In some instances, weather presents greater challenges today than it did a hundred years ago, particularly in winter. Before the automobile era snow was more easily dealt with. One either stayed put during a blizzard and its aftermath or took to sleighs. Daily long-distance commutes were, of course, unknown. An inescapable conclusion from reading town histories is that fire was a continual and constant menace. Meetinghouses, hotels, stores and houses seem to have been destroyed by fires and rebuilt within months almost as a matter of course. Firefighting was rudimentary at best; little equipment was available and by the time it got to where it was needed, it was usually too late.

The flood of 1936 is less well remembered today, having been overshadowed by the 1938 hurricane. It occurred in March and was particularly destructive because of the ice-laden rivers. The W.S. Farnsworth store in Peterborough was so damaged that it had to be demolished. It was located at the corner of Main and Summer Streets. The site is still vacant. (PHS)

101

Viewing the flood waters from in front of the Unitarian Church in Peterborough. The hurricane and the fire that followed destroyed the block of Main Street from Depot Street to the river, seen here on September 21, 1938. (PHS)

The sandbags placed across Grove Street in Peterborough don't seem to have helped much. School Street enters from the left. (PHS)

Main Street, Jaffrey, on September 21, 1938. The Jaffrey Mills are on the right. The bridge was not re-opened until the following year. (JHS)

Marlborough during the 1938 hurricane. The Blanket Mill is on the left, the old fire station in the center. Every town in the region was affected and for several days after the great storm each was almost totally isolated from the outside world. (MHS)

A cyclone hit West Rindge on September 15, 1928. Shown here is the basket company on the left, the store, and the post office. The store now houses the basket company. (RHS)

The firemen of New Ipswich pictured some time in the 1890s with the Hunneman pumper "Southern Hero," which had been purchased in 1860. The building is the Smith Village fire station, since moved and now a residence. (NIHS)

104

The Fourth Congregational Church in New Ipswich, destroyed by fire after a lightning strike on July 15, 1902. Built in 1812, it was used as the town meetinghouse until 1832. The 1,116-pound Paul Revere bell was destroyed in the fire. The church was rebuilt and dedicated in 1903. (NIHS)

"Tiger No. 1" outside the New Ipswich Historical Society building (formerly Schoolhouse No. 1) where it now resides. The pumper, also made by the William Hunneman Co. in Boston and delivered in 1860, served the town until the 1920s when motorized equipment was purchased. Pictured are John Preston, James Barr and Charles Pratt. (NIHS)

Peterborough's Tarbell Block on the corner of Main and Grove Streets was heavily damaged by fire on December 7, 1902. It was renovated with an extra two floors added and is now known as the Granite Block. (PHS)

"Aquarius," one of Peterborough's earliest pieces of fire apparatus, was purchased in 1857 for around $700. It has been restored and is in the fire museum on Summer Street. The hose reel is on the left in the entranceway. (PHS)

Peterborough's new American La France fire engine, delivered in 1915. The Main Street fire station still stands but has since been converted to offices and apartments. The present-day fire station is on Summer Street. (PHS)

The Peterborough fire department in the early 1900s in front of "Aquarius," probably at a firemen's muster. The letter A on their uniforms is for Aquarius which was the early name of the fire company before it became a department of town government. (PHS)

Marlborough's old fire station, built in 1867, at the intersection of South Main and East Main Streets, a stretch called Engine Hill. It was razed in 1967 due to the reconstruction of Route 101. The tower to the left was used for drying hoses. Behind is the steeple of the Universalist Church. (MHS)

The old Methodist Church ablaze on February 28, 1933. It survived but burned again in 1947 with the loss of the steeple. It is now the Community House on Marlborough's Main Street. (MHS)

Six

Moving About:
From the
Horse to the Car

Transport was always a prime consideration in the early days of life in the Monadnock region. Only supporting the church and providing schooling received more attention than the building and maintaining of roads. The towns and settlements that were so isolated and insular in the mid-1750s have in the 1990s become part of the global village. The rough foot trails through the forest became roads, barely passable in most instances; then the turnpikes of the early 1800s were developed, followed by the railroad beginning in the mid-1800s. It was the railroad that really opened the region to the rest of the world and allowed the establishment and growth of the mill economy and the tourist trade. But the biggest change, the one with the most far-reaching effects, was the arrival of the automobile.

Pictured here in 1890 is the stable at Cutter's Hotel in Jaffrey. On the left is Jonas Cutter; on the right, P.J. Quinn. The sitting gentleman is unidentified. Just as with the car today, the horse required an array of support services: the stable, the feed dealer, the blacksmith, the saddle and harness maker, the wheelwright and the carriage builder. Cutter's Hotel burned in 1901. (JHS)

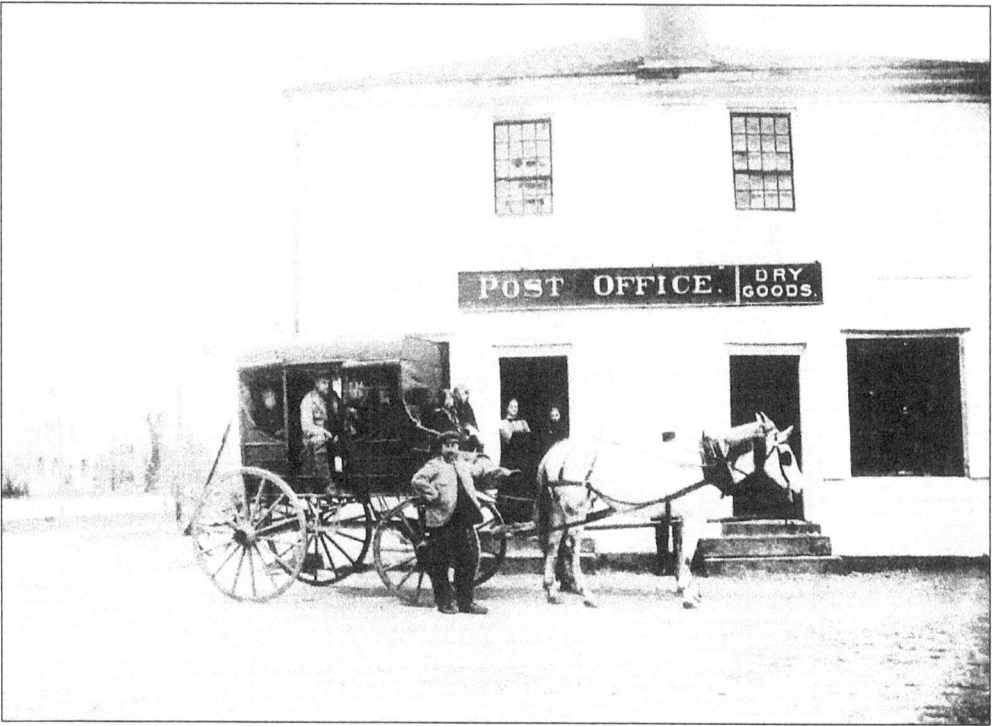

A stagecoach in front of the Corner Store in New Ipswich. The store was also the post office between 1861 and 1933. Torn down in 1946, it was at the corner of Main Street and Route 124. (NIHS)

A two-horse wagon of the Harrisville & Dublin Stage Company driven by George Knowlton, c. 1880. Behind is the Mason store in Dublin and to the right, the Community (First Congregational) Church. (HHI)

A rural postman delivering by carriage, possibly in Jaffrey. Now motorized, rural delivery remains an important link in the communication system of the Monadnock region. (JHS)

Before roads were paved they needed to be watered in the summer to keep down the dust. Peterborough's sprinkler wagon, driven by Alvin Townsend, is seen here at the corner of Grove and School Streets. (PHS)

Ernest Wilson beside F.M. Roberts' "meat wagon" in 1912 in New Ipswich. It made the rounds of the town every Wednesday and Saturday. (NIHS)

Ambrose L. Shattuck was in the ice business in Peterborough for forty-six years beginning in 1873. Most of his ice was cut from Cunningham Pond. (PHS)

Winter was the season for working in the woods. The ground was frozen, the leaves were gone (as were the insects) and it was easier hauling over snow than mud or rock. C.A. Blood is holding the reins in this 1907 winter logging scene in New Ipswich. (NIHS)

Fred A. Shirland's delivery sleigh in New Ipswich around 1907. Shirland ran the grocery store in Smith Village. (NIHS)

The postal sleigh at the Hancock Post Office in 1902. Charles Turner of Stoddard is the driver and in front of the door is the postmaster, Edgar Ware. The post office building is now a residence on Main Street. (HHS)

Dublin's snowroller in front of the Mason store and the Community (First Congregational) Church. Rather than plowing, as is done today, the main roads were rolled to improve the surface for sleighing. (DHS)

The New Ipswich snowroller on Route 124, photographed on February 4, 1913. The house on the right with Gothic revival details is easily identified today a few hundred yards east of the Main Street intersection. (NIHS)

The R.M. Lawrence livery stable on Main Street in Marlborough. The stable was connected to the building on the left, the Marlborough Hotel. They were both destroyed by fire in 1970. On the site now is Doody's Mini Mart. Note the trolley tracks in the foreground. (MHS)

George Farrar, seen behind the seatback, was a Peterborough farrier and wagon maker. The carriage's unusual design probably prompted the photograph. Farrar's shop is now the Sandhill store on Grove Street. (PHS)

The coming of the railroad changed the Monadnock region in many fundamental ways. Of course, it improved access and speeded communication, both for people and for businesses. It also allowed the mill economy that had been steadily developing since the early 1800s to expand explosively in a manner it could never have done in the days of horse-drawn transportation. Markets could now be broadened to cover the country and even the world. Tourism was given a great boost by the railroad; hotels and boarding houses were now within easy reach of the eastern cities.

The region's first rail lines were built in the 1840s, linking Boston and Keene and greatly benefiting Fitzwilliam, Troy and Marlborough. In the 1870s the railroad was extended from Winchendon to Rindge, Jaffrey and Peterborough. Lines served Hancock and Harrisville, too. Towns vied with one another for rail service, paying to the railroads a specified portion of their property valuation for the privilege. Having the railroad come to town meant having a depot, which also often meant new commercial development and activity around the depot.

The Rindge station, pictured here, was sited in Blakeville, renamed West Rindge at the urging of the railroad. This view is toward Jaffrey. The station burned sometime before 1920 but was rebuilt. In 1958 passenger service was discontinued, and in the 1970s the tracks here and in Jaffrey and Peterborough were removed. (RHS)

The Peterborough Depot was built about 1871 and stood until 1961, quite naturally, on Depot Street near what is now the Toadstool Bookstore. (PHS)

Another view of the Peterborough Depot showing the Needham Basket Company on the left. (PHS)

118

The Troy railroad station on Water Street. Visitors to Mount Monadnock, particularly those going to the Mountain House, would use this station and continue on by carriage. When Henry David Thoreau visited Monadnock he arrived at the station on June 2, 1858. He and his companion shouldered their knapsacks and walked the 4 miles to the mountain. The station has since been converted to housing. (WH)

The railroad station at Marlborough, located at the top of Water Street. Built in 1878, it was abandoned sixty years later. Two lines ran through Marlborough: the first, between Keene and Boston, opened in 1848. The Webb Depot served the granite quarries. The second line was opened in 1878 and ran between Keene and Manchester, with stations also at Harrisville and Hancock. (MHS)

Built in 1878, the Hancock Depot was located a short distance from the village. After it closed down it was used as a camp building until—in 1979—it was moved to a new site nearby. Over a ten-year period, it was renovated by the volunteer members of the Hancock Depot Association and today it is used for cultural and educational purposes. (HHS)

Elmwood Depot was an important junction for two rail lines that intersected in the eastern part of Hancock: the Manchester and Keene Railroad and the Peterborough and Hillsborough Railroad. By the early 1940s both lines had been closed. (HHS)

The Harrisville station in 1907. It was served by the Manchester and Keene Railroad. The building still stands although the covered platform has been removed. (HHI)

Although much altered the Jaffrey Depot still stands just south of Main Street. Rail service from Winchendon commenced in 1870. Up until 1887 wood was used for the locomotives and huge woodsheds were maintained at the station. (JHS)

The first locomotive to arrive in Peterborough. The line, extended from Jaffrey, opened to traffic on June 6, 1871. (PHS)

The 1000-foot-long wood trestle over Alcock's Ravine in Hancock on the Manchester and Keene line. Seventy-five feet high, it followed a curving alignment. It was replaced by an iron trestle in the mid-1880s. (HHS)

The Newell trestle, also in Hancock. It too was originally fabricated of wood. The granite piers and abutments can still be seen from the Old Harrisville Road. Newell's Mill which stood close by was later owned and operated by Harry M. Sheldon who turned out, amongst other things, tent pegs and clothespins. (HHS)

The trestle in Marlborough near Little Canada. Of a very similar design to the Newell trestle—they were both on the Manchester and Keene line—it was taken down during World War II. (MHS)

The only town in the region served by a trolley line was Marlborough. Workers are shown here in 1900 during construction along Main Street, near Water Street. It ran from Keene and terminated close to the Collins' store, now the pizza parlor. (MHS)

A Keene Electric Railway trolley car on Main Street in front of the Methodist Church. The line was abandoned in 1926. (MHS)

An early car, possibly a 1909 Buick, in front of New Ipswich's Union Hall and Watatic Grange, next to the New Ipswich Historical Society building on Main Street. The Grange, built c. 1840, still stands but is used very infrequently. (NIHS)

A Public Service Company work party in the 1920s shown somewhere in Marlborough. The man second from the left is Alfred Beaudoin. (MHS)

Fred Ames and his crew with an early steamroller used in the rebuilding of Concord Street in Peterborough. (PHS)

This collection of early automobiles is interesting; so are the drivers and passengers. The gentlemen are the so-called "Peterborough Elders of 1930." The inspiration for their selection was the "Apostolic Twelve," Peterborough citizens thought picturesque by an itinerant photographer in the 1870s. The resulting photographic portraits were displayed in The Tavern for more than seventy-five years. The man standing is A. Erland Goyette. (PHS)

Roscoe Sawyer, one of a long line of Jaffrey Sawyers, leaving his dairy on a local home delivery run in 1933. The Sawyer family today operates Jaffrey's last dairy farm. (JHS)

The notation on the back of this snapshot reads "Probably the first auto wreck in Jaffrey, on the Ark Road." The car on the right labeled "Dillon" may have been that of Edward or Oscar Dillon, father and son, who ran an auto livery service for many years. (JHS)

Acknowledgments

In contemplating this book it immediately became obvious that the local historical societies of the Monadnock region would be the richest source of old photographs recording the life, development and changes over time of this special area of New Hampshire. As a resident of Jaffrey and an active member of both the Jaffrey Historical Society and the Village Improvement Society, the author saw the preparation of this book as an opportunity to bring the societies of the neighboring towns together in a co-operative enterprise that among other things might have the beneficial effect of advancing the knowledge and appreciation of the history and heritage of our individual communities, and of the region as a whole. A considerable amount of time and effort was spent by historical society members in compiling this collection of early views, in assisting in the necessary research and in offering advice and encouragement.

The author would like to extend his heartfelt thanks to the following societies and the individuals who have participated in this effort and who have allowed their photographs to appear in this book:

Dublin Historical Society (DHS): John W. Harris, Nancy E. Campbell.
Fitzwilliam Historical Society (FHS): Jean Camden, Barbara Crutchley, Robert J. Corrette.
Hancock Historical Society (HHS): Gloria J. Neary.
Historic Harrisville, Inc. (HHI): Mary Meath, John J. Colony III, Whitney Fletcher.
Jaffrey Center Village Improvement Society (VIS): Mary R. Payson.
Jaffrey Historical Society (JHS): William M. Driscoll, Owen R. Houghton, Scott Cunningham.
Marlborough Historical Society (MHS): Richard and Jane Butler, Priscilla L. Richardson, Philip Clark.
New Ipswich Historical Society (NIHS): Mary O. Hall, Patricia G. Hoffman.
Peterborough Historical Society (PHS): Ellen S. Derby.
Rindge Historical Society (RHS): Linda Bussiere, Ralph Hoyt.
Private Collections: Warian T. Hawkins (WH); H. Charles Royce (HCR); Robert B. Stephenson (RBS).

Note: The initials in parentheses may be used to identify the source of each photograph.

www.ingramcontent.com/pod-product-compliance
Lightning Source LLC
Chambersburg PA
CBHW080909100426
42812CB00007B/2221